# JUSTIN BIEBER

## CONFIDENTIAL

First edition for North America published in 2014
by Barron's Educational Series, Inc.

All inquiries should be addressed to:
Barron's Educational Series, Inc.
250 Wireless Boulevard,
Hauppauge, New York 11788
www.barronseduc.com

ISBN: 978-1-4380-0501-0

Library of Congress Control Number: 2013955116

Date of Manufacture: December 2013
Manufactured by: Oriental Press, Dubai, UAE

Printed in Dubai, UAE

10 9 8 7 6 5 4 3 2 1

# JUSTIN BIEBER

## CONFIDENTIAL

UNAUTHORIZED

**BARRON'S**

# CONTENTS

**LEFT**
*Justin takes center stage on his*
Believe Tour, *Barclays Center,*
*New York, August 2, 2013.*

# INTRODUCTION

It's been one of the biggest, most spectacular, and successful tours in the modern music world. *The Believe Tour*, which ran from September 2012 to December 2013, crossed North and South America, Europe, Asia, Australasia, and South Africa. The show at Madison Square Garden in New York City sold out in 22 seconds. At the beginning of each show, the singer hovers down from the top of the stage, wearing wings, and remains there, soaking up the screams and applause for thirty seconds. "It's such a big moment," he's said. "I think people will remember that! People are just captivated…"

**LEFT**
*Flying in on his famous silver wings to wow the Nottingham, England, Capital FM Arena audience, March 2, 2013.*

The singer is, of course, Justin Bieber, and the world has been captivated by his big moments for some years now. Still only 19, the Canadian star rose to fame with dizzying speed and just continues to break records and dominate the pop scene. Albums such as *My World* and *Believe* have sold many millions worldwide. His movie *Never Say Never* dazzled audiences. He has collected huge earnings, awards, and GRAMMY nominations. In 2012, *Forbes* magazine named him the third most powerful celebrity in the world. He has over 46 million followers on Twitter and three billion views on YouTube—more than anyone else alive—and a feverishly loyal army of fans, known, of course, as "Beliebers." Biebermania and Bieberholics follow wherever he goes.

How did this giddy ascent come about? You'll know some of the rise-of-the-underdog story from the biopic-documentary *Never Say Never*. As recently as January 19, 2007, Justin's mother uploaded the first video of her son singing and performing to YouTube. She expected a few friends and family members to be interested, but it led to so much more than anybody could have imagined. Suddenly, young Justin was carried from his small home city to the pinnacles of the U.S. music industry, as record companies saw in him something as stellar and special as his hero Michael Jackson. Before you could say "Baby,"

*" I guess you can say that I've been blessed with talent. "*

JUSTIN BIEBER

**ABOVE**

*The gang's all here: Justin with his dad, Jeremy; his mom, Pattie; and little sister, Jazmyn, 2011.*

he was—releasing his first single at 15—possibly the hottest sensation since The King of Pop himself.

Speaking of babies, Justin Drew Bieber was born on March 1, 1994, at 12:56 AM, in a Canadian city called London. He grew up in Stratford, another small city, in the province of Ontario. Before he was fully aware of the way the press and media work, and watching his words more carefully, he said, "Nothing ever came out of Stratford." Millions of Bieber fans would surely disagree! The population there is around thirty thousand, and, in fact, one famed gentleman did live there once—Thomas Edison, inventor of the light bulb. Little did Justin, in early childhood, realize that his own fame would one day light up the lives of Beliebers like a billion light bulbs!

He wasn't the only good-looking thing there. When Justin was 3-years-old, the quiet, peaceful Stratford was voted "the prettiest city in the world." It took its name from the well-known English town of Stratford-upon-Avon, legendary for being the birthplace of William Shakespeare, and celebrates the connection with a theatrical festival in honor of the playwright every year. Justin used to perform outside one of the theaters!

His parents, Jeremy and Pattie (who was 18 when Justin was born), married in 1992: it has been said he has the eyes and nose of his father and the mouth of his mother. Sadly, their marriage failed and they divorced. While Jeremy (himself a singer-musician) moved to Winnipeg in Manitoba, Pattie, gaining full custody of their son, stayed in Stratford (where she'd grown up). Justin kept his dad's last name, but his mom reverted to her maiden name, Pattie Mallette. As a single mother, she struggled financially. She and Justin lived in public housing in one of the less well-off areas of Stratford. "We were living below the poverty line," Pattie, then an aspiring actress, said. "We struggled. I worked two jobs just to make ends meet. But we had all the essentials."

Years later, in an interview with Canadian magazine *Maclean's*, Justin recalled, "Some people have it misconstrued. I mean, I wasn't... "poor." I definitely didn't think of myself as not having a lot of money. I couldn't afford to get new clothes a lot of times, but I had a roof over my

*" We struggled. I worked two jobs just to make ends meet. But we had all the essentials. "*

PATTIE, JUSTIN'S MOM

LEFT
*Proud mom Pattie Mallette.*

head. I was very fortunate. I had my grandparents, too. I saw a lot of them and they were very kind. So I grew up getting everything that I wanted."

One friend has described him as "a comedian, a joker, a smart aleck. He liked to mess around, to get a reaction." He sang in the church band, taking an early interest in music. He'd dabble on the organ and keyboards there. "People would show me stuff and I'd try to do what they did," he's said. "I just liked music. I really had a passion for it." He also enjoyed the music of Michael Jackson ("My mom listened to him and I watched him on YouTube") and Stevie Wonder. Boyz II Men were another favorite. "My mom would play their album over and over, and I'd go to my bedroom and try to do those vocal acrobatics." He was even playing drums—on pots and pans—when he was two! By the time he was four, his mother was fed up with him banging out beats on the furniture and bought him a drum set, with help from the church, who had taken a collection especially for this. Little did they know what they were launching! To avoid the wrath of neighbors, Justin's drum set was kept in his grandparents' cellar, and that's where he practiced for hours and hours. As Justin is left-handed, he had to be extra-skillful to adapt to the right-handed drum set. He persevered, determined, and one of the videos on his YouTube channel shows him mastering his percussive techniques with great dexterity.

Hungry now to learn and play more instruments, he progressed to teaching himself to play guitar, piano, and trumpet. "I guess you can say I've been blessed with talent," he declared. His grandmother helped him with the piano; his mother found him a secondhand guitar when he was six. On his MySpace page, he later wrote, "I just grew up around music my whole

*Justin's father, Jeremy, August 2012.*

" *My mom would play the Boyz II Men album over and over, and I'd go to my bedroom and try to do those vocal acrobatics.* "

JUSTIN BIEBER

life. I would sing around the house. It was just kind of a thing that I loved to do." His other major hobby was hockey. His sports idol was ice-hockey star Wayne Gretsky. Justin supported the Toronto Maple Leafs. He threw himself into games, and his grandfather has said, "He's always been energetic. You had to keep him going all the time. He had to be in sports all the time, or if not, he was bouncing off the walls." A typical Pisces, some might say. Justin's always said that if he hadn't made it in music, he would have loved to be a hockey player, although he's also suggested he could have been a chef —"to cook all the lovely ladies a nice dinner."

Justin was homeschooled by Pattie between kindergarten and first grade, then attended the Jeanne Sauve Catholic School and the Stratford Northwestern Public School. A teacher there has said, "He has no fear. I couldn't believe how quickly he could pick things up." Justin recalled his first kiss at 13 while slow dancing during a school dance. Indeed, his dancing was blossoming, too, as evidenced by a YouTube clip of him showing off his break-dancing moves at just 8 years old. Less successfully, his first date ended with him spilling spaghetti and meatballs all over himself! "She never went out with me again. It was terrible and embarrassing. So I would suggest NOT going out for Italian on a first date because it can be messy —I'll never make that mistake again!"

**RIGHT**
*Justin takes his mom to the 40th Anniversary of the American Music Awards. The singer was nominated for three awards, November 18, 2012.*

**BELOW**
*Justin attends the Pencils of Promise 2011 charity gala at Espace, New York, November 17, 2011.*

# BIEBER FACTS!

JUSTIN SUPPORTS MORE THAN 20 CHARITIES. AMONG THEM, PENCILS FOR PROMISE, FOUNDED BY HIS MANAGER SCOOTER'S YOUNGER BROTHER, ADAM BRAUN. IT BUILDS SCHOOLS IN DEVELOPING COUNTRIES, AND JUSTIN TAKES PART IN FUND-RAISING GALAS AND DONATES MONEY FROM HIS CONCERTS.

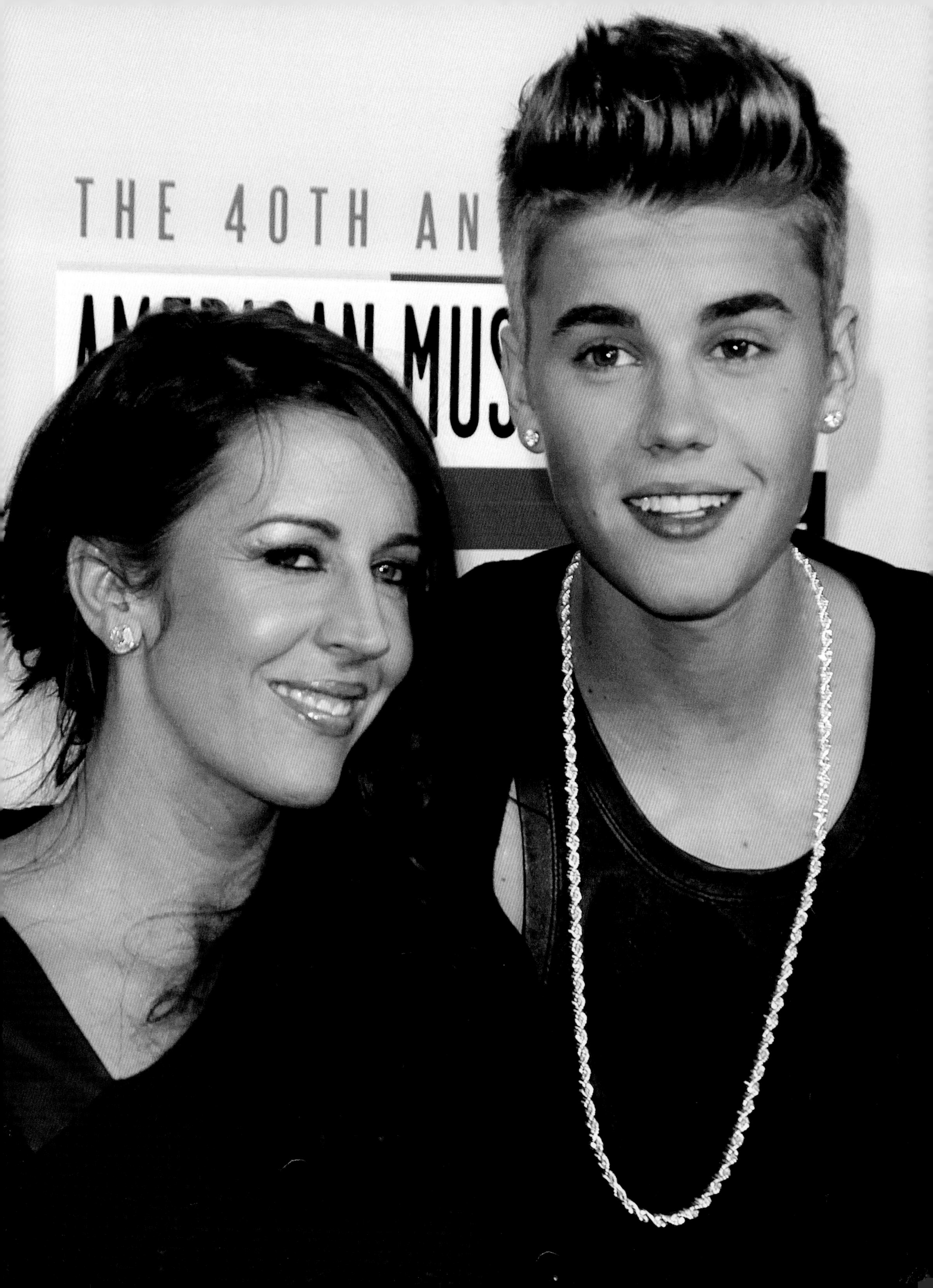
THE 40TH AN

"I've been to a lot of places around the world," he's said recently, "but my favorite place is still my home town." He loved the snowy winters, and he loved performing with his guitar. Incredibly, at 13, he made so much money from street performing that he was able to take his mom on vacation to Florida. Right there is an example of his work ethic and ability to charm. Soon mastering the trumpet and singing in the church choir, he was bursting to take things further. In 2007, he signed up to enter a competition, Stratford Star (similiar to *American Idol*). "The other people had been taking singing lessons and had vocal coaches," he's recalled. "I wasn't taking it too seriously at times. I just did it for fun, not to be famous or anything." Justin sang Sarah McLachlan's song "Angel," then Aretha Franklin's "Respect," while dancing and playing air-saxophone with abandon. Next he offered Alicia Keys' "Fallin'" and "Numbers" by Matchbox Twenty and Lil' Bow Wow, and then Ne-Yo's "So Sick." The judges put him through to the final three—among much older, more experienced contestants—but he ultimately lost to Kirsten Hawley. Regardless, his confidence was boosted and he sang at local events more and more. "That's when I figured out I really wanted to sing; it was my passion."

His mother, too, was boosted. She wanted to share the videos of Justin's performances with friends and relatives, and so she utilized YouTube. Justin's account was called "kidrauhl." "We put my singing videos from the competition there so that my friends and family could watch them," remembered Justin, "but it turned out that other people liked them too." And then some! His videos became a global Internet sensation. "I was like, oh, I don't have 100 people in my family. And then, oh, I don't have 500 people in my family. And… it just kept getting bigger and bigger." Justin Bieber's fame and popularity were about to get bigger than he could ever have imagined.

 **RIGHT**
*Proud son thanks his mom, Pattie, onstage at the American Music Awards after winning the prestigious Artist of the Year, November 18, 2012. The pair were later seen dancing the night away!*

# BREAKTHROUGH

Justin Bieber has sung about Cinderella in one of his songs, and, in many ways, his is a Cinderella story. Every teenage wannabe pop star dreams of being discovered, plucked from millions of hopefuls, and given the opportunity to shine in the pop world. Fortunately for his countless admirers, Justin was. He seized the chance with both hands, and hasn't looked back since.

**RIGHT**
*Dreams come true: Justin and his idol, Usher, perform onstage during Z100's Jingle Ball at Madison Square Garden, New York, December 11, 2009.*

**BELOW**
*The singer with manager Scooter Braun, October 2010.*

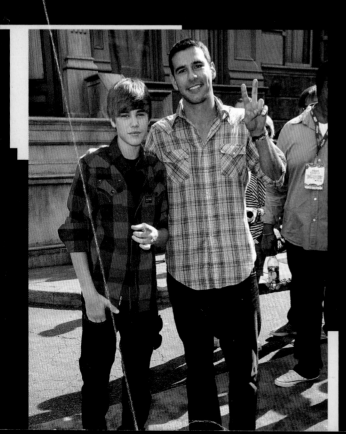

**AS MORE AND MORE PEOPLE CLICKED ON HIS YOUTUBE VIDEOS,** record companies, managers, and talent scouts perked up and took notice, wondering if Justin could be the next big thing. His mother, Pattie, was justifiably wary and cautious: if Justin was going to sign a record deal, she wanted everything about it to feel right.

"I was contacted by many different record executives, and a lot of different managers and agents," Justin later told a Canadian magazine. "My mom basically said: 'Justin, I don't think this is going to happen, it's not going to work. We don't have a lawyer, or money for a lawyer, and we're not going to sign something if we don't know what it says.' So we ended up just declining all these people." Yet it wasn't that Pattie didn't want success for her son. He just had to be patient.

And then the right man with the right attitude and approach came along. Scott Braun—known as Scooter Braun—had been highly impressed by Justin's online performances, especially his interpretation of Ne-Yo's "So Sick." He professed to being "blown away" that "a little kid had a range like that." He joked, "So then I stalked him."

**ABOVE**
*Adam Braun, Usher, and Scooter attend the Pencils of Promise Gala, October 2012.*

**RIGHT**
*Usher and his protégé at the Nickelodeon Kids' Choice Awards, March 28, 2009.*

**" I was looking for someone who was like Michael Jackson. Someone who captivated not only kids but adults, too. "** SCOOTER BRAUN

# BIEBER FACTS!

**JUSTIN CAN SOLVE A RUBIK'S CUBE WITHIN TWO MINUTES, AND HE ONCE SIGNED FIFTY POSTERS IN THREE MINUTES.**

Born in 1982, Braun had learned his trade as an events organizer, working for rapper Ludacris as he supported Eminem on tour. He found a niche in the music industry and was hired by producer Jermaine Dupri (who had produced Usher and Mariah Carey) to work for his record label, So So Def Records. Soon he'd climbed to the title of Executive Director of Marketing, though his less formal nickname was "hustla." He hung out with the likes of Kanye West and Britney Spears. In 2004 he left, aged 23, to form his own company, SB Projects, an entertainment and promotions company, which involved him in music, movies, and television projects. He quickly became a very powerful figure. He signed MC Asher Roth and helped his debut album into the U.S. top five. Now he was looking for the "next Michael Jackson." "I wanted someone who was like Michael," he said. "Someone who captivated not only kids but adults, too." Step forward young Bieber.

DOLCE & GABBANA
DOLCE & GABBANA
PENCILS OF PROMISE
DOLCE & GABBANA

One night Scooter was checking out a new talent recommended by Akon on YouTube and a few clicks later found himself watching Justin singing Aretha Franklin's "Respect." "It was such raw talent, my gut just went wild!" he exclaimed. He felt compelled to watch more of Justin's videos. "I was really impressed with how young he was and how he was holding the crowd with his guitar. I said: 'I need to find this kid!'" He tracked down Justin's family via his school board and began trying to persuade Pattie that he was the right man to oversee her son's rise to fame. At first, according to Justin, Pattie just tried to get rid of him!

Justin later told *Billboard*, "He was very persistent. He even called my great aunt." Eventually Scooter and Pattie spoke on the phone, for hours. They agreed to meet. "And it turned out he was a cool guy," added Justin. "A great guy, a really solid guy."

Mother and son were flown out to Atlanta, Georgia to meet Braun informally and to visit his recording studios. Demos would be made. Justin hung out with his Svengali-to-be and despite the 12-year age difference, they bonded. Both were determined, energetic, ambitious. And as they arrived at the studios by car, they bumped into another man who was to prove significant in Bieber's breakthrough—R&B superstar Usher. "He was going into the studio the same time as me and I ran up to him as fast as I could," recalled Justin. He told Usher he was a huge fan of his music. He must have made an impact, because within a week Usher was checking out his YouTube videos and, after discussions with Scooter, decided he wanted to sign him. Usher and Scooter flew Justin out to Atlanta again, and this time Justin sang live for one of his idols. Indeed, he chose to do an Usher chart-topping song, "U Got It Bad." "You gonna sing it with me, or what?" he teased Usher, halfway through. His comment made Usher laugh. He knew Justin was unique.

Pattie filmed the performance, and Justin took delight in showing his school pals that he hadn't invented their meeting. That video has since been watched by many millions on Justin's YouTube channel. Usher has declared, "When I met him, his personality just won me over. And then when he sang, I realized we were dealing with the real thing. His voice just spoke to the type of music I would want to be associated with. It was magical." Justin remained relatively relaxed about the potential record deal, claiming he had nothing to lose. "I was just there having fun. If you're not having fun, why do it?" Usher

**LEFT**
*Justin takes requests at the Nintendo World Store, New York, August 31, 2009.*

**ABOVE**
*Up close and personal with excited fans at the Nintendo World Store.*

**"** When I met him, his personality just won me over.
And then when he sang, I realized we were dealing
with the real thing. **"** USHER

was convinced. "I immediately knew that this kid was poised to be a star," he told the Canadian press. "I knew that I had a lot to offer him, based on where I'd been… my experience. I just wanted to help him tell his story. I just felt: you know, this is the one. He's going to be huge. He's going to be massive. That's all I can say."

He and Scooter weren't the only ones feeling it now. Before Usher could put a deal on the table, Braun had also notified others of his discovery. Among these was Justin Timberlake, the hugely popular GRAMMY-winning pop star and actor, who also had a label. He was suitably impressed, and "100% in." Justin Bieber met Justin Timberlake and the Hollywood star's then-girlfriend Jessica Biel, when he went to their home to watch a basketball game with them. Pattie said, "Justin Timberlake also wanted to sign him, so it became almost like a bidding war between them. Two of the biggest pop stars, wanting

**LEFT**
*Justin meets two of his youngest fans, and reads a lunchtime story, at the Read for the Record campaign event, New York, October 8, 2009.*

**ABOVE**
*Signing autographs for delirious fans at the Hard Rock Cafe, Las Vegas, October 24, 2009.*

*Wowing the snap-happy crowd
at the Hard Rock Cafe, Las Vegas,
October 24, 2009.*

to be involved with my little Justin!" Her little Justin wisely deduced that this contest between two rivals was a win-win situation for him. "It was just crazy," he recalled. "Justin was a great guy. They're both great." The way they went, it transpired, was with Usher. "I hope to collaborate with Justin [Timberlake] in the future," said Bieber afterward.

He signed to Raymond Braun Media Group, Scooter and Usher's joint venture. Usher's contact L.A. Reid then snapped him up to Island/Def Jam Records, in October 2008. Usher's then-manager Chris Hicks was appointed to Vice President of Def Jam, in order to oversee Justin's career at the label. Braun officially became Justin's manager (and chief advisor). He felt that Justin signing with a black artist and an R&B-led label and team would convey to the record-buying public that Justin's forte was soul and R&B music. "Here's

this little white kid from Canada singing soul music," he said. "He needed someone to make people understand that's who he really was… his talent is undeniable." Usher would be Justin's mentor. "Stay humble and stay on the right path," he advised. "Then anything's possible." Braun made a bold prediction. "Justin's going to be the first artist to become a huge mainstream superstar based on the Internet and not on anything else."

To stay on top of this whirlwind of activity, and to begin recording sessions, Justin and his mother moved temporarily to Atlanta. "He's got a long journey and great plans ahead," said Pattie. Swiftly, he was the most-subscribed-to YouTube musician in Canada, and ranked twentieth in the world. And by July 2009, Justin's first single was out. Life would never be the same.

**BIEBER FACTS!**

HIS FAVORITE NUMBER IS SIX AND HIS FAVORITE COLOR IS PURPLE.

**LEFT**
*Appearing on the famous Today Show on TV to millions of his U.S. fans, October 12, 2009.*

**ABOVE**
*Unplugged and performing live on Good Morning America, New York, November 15, 2009.*

# FAME

Some teenage boys might have been intimidated by moving to Atlanta and entering the recording studio with giants of the business. Not Justin Bieber, who wasn't lacking in "swag." "I really love to be in the spotlight and just be the center of attention," he admitted. The time for demos was over: now he and his supportive team were looking to record hits. He collaborated with leading writers and producers such as Tricky Stewart, Bryan-Michael Cox, Terius "the Dream" Nash, Johntá Austin, and Kuk Harrell. He listened and learned fast; Usher and Scooter were there with guidance and suggestions whenever necessary.

Usher became almost an "older brother" figure. Scooter said, "He's very protective of Justin. He sees himself at that age, and doesn't want Justin

*So close! Justin's fans reach out to tou their idol, December 22, 2009.*

making any of the mistakes he made. He wants him to win!" Justin went go-karting and to movies with the mentor he described as his "big brother." He found relocating from Canada reasonably stress-free. He said to MTV, "In my town there were only thirty thousand people, and everybody knows everybody. But in Atlanta there are millions—and I don't know anybody!"

The all-important debut single was written by Stewart and Nash, whose track record included such global smash hits as Rihanna's "Umbrella" and Beyoncé's "Single Ladies (Put A Ring On It)." The former had also penned hits for Mariah Carey and Britney Spears. So Justin had every cause to be optimistic! They delivered a song titled "One Time." And from the opening beats and Justin's high chant of "me, plus you," all involved knew they were onto a winner. The song's theme of true undying love naturally found a place in the hearts of girls around the world. "I love singing about love," Justin told

"I really love to be in the spotlight and just be the center of attention. "
JUSTIN BIEBER

**ABOVE**
A trip back home to Canada sees JB offer roses to a fan at MuchMusic Studios, Toronto, December 22, 2009.

Twist magazine. "That's what a lot of girls like listening to, and that's what I like to write." At his age, it may have been puppy love, but his fans understood and embraced that. "It's just a fun pop record," Justin added.

Promotional activities began with more online videos and messages. A full video, shot at Usher's house and guest-starring its owner, was directed by Vashtie Kola. "He's super-talented and more street than any of these child stars!" she enthused. *Billboard* reviewed "One Time" with positivity, reckoning it "gives Bieber's vocals plenty of room to shine, especially when the young singer confidently breaks into the chorus, connecting overtly with his fans." It was also reviewed as "a perfect kick-off," "a hallmark pop song that taps into a prevalent teen-pop aesthetic," "hip hop inflected," and "already an online sensation." *Entertainment Weekly* declared it a "refreshingly age-appropriate chronicle of young love."

**ABOVE**
*Fifteen years old and rocking on the Today Show, October 12, 2009.*

**RIGHT**
*Usher and Justin attend TNT's Christmas in Washington at the National Building Museum, December 13, 2009.*

"One Time" climbed the charts, slowly but surely. It almost made the top 20 on the *Billboard* chart, and the top ten in Canada (where it went platinum, selling ten thousand copies). It also made considerable inroads in Europe and elsewhere. Justin was up and running! "That was not luck," he had quipped in the video. "That was skill!" When he heard his song on the radio for the first time in his mom's car, he exclaimed, "That was pretty weird!"

He'd soon get used to the weirdness. Things accelerated beyond anyone's expectations. Even before his debut album emerged, he set a new record as the first solo artist ever to have four songs from a debut album appear on *Billboard*'s Hot 100 before the album had been released. "One Time" was followed in October by "One Less Lonely Girl," co-written by Usher, where Justin famously announces, "OK—let's go!" and concludes, chuckling, "Only you, shorty!" The video featured him falling for a girl he spotted at the laundromat, flirty smiles in full flow. The third (digital-only) single was "Love Me," and the fourth was the up-tempo "Favorite Girl," rumored to be directed at his new friend, fast-rising country-pop singer Taylor Swift. In fact, Justin dedicated it to her on a YouTube video, but then shrewdly added, "Don't worry, ladies, you're all my favorite girl, ha ha ha!" He performed the song on TV on *The Ellen DeGeneres Show*. The well-known host introduced

# BIEBER FACTS!

JUSTIN'S PET MONKEY IS A CAPUCHIN MONKEY AND IS NAMED MALLY, AFTER THE PRODUCER MALLY MALL, WHO GAVE IT TO HIM.

him enthusiastically: "Our next guest has a mind-boggling 80 million views on YouTube and he's only 15 years old. Please welcome the adorable Justin Bieber!" The audience was overflowing with excitable Bieber fans. "You have the talent, the charisma," Ellen told him. "I couldn't imagine you getting cuter. But this business is crazy, a rollercoaster, so stay really grounded."

If he could hardly take in what was happening and how popular he had become so quickly, he was about to see everything race up another gear or three. Not yet 16, he looked forward to his first album's release. And, in November 2009, the seven-track *My World* did not disappoint, with all its tracks charting and the "extended play" going platinum. It was just a taste, though. With fans eager for more, studio recording continued, and in March 2010 the full-length studio album *My World 2.0* was released. It, too, went platinum, going straight to number one in many countries and giving us the enormous hit "Baby." Justin was now one of the most talked-about names on the face of the earth. His fans all around the planet were desperate to see him perform. It was time for his first major tour, and Justin wanted to present those fans with an experience they'd never forget.

# MY WORLD

The world was now Justin Bieber's oyster. As his studio calling card, and proof that he could cut it recording-wise, *My World* came in two chapters. Initially, the seven-track EP came out, then *My World 2.0*, both establishing him high in the charts and going platinum. *My World* went double platinum in the U.K. The singles "One Time" and "One Less Lonely Girl" familiarized themselves with the U.S. top ten. Justin spoke of "songs that teens can relate to" and said they covered "stuff that happens in everyday life."

**RIGHT**
*Shining silver like a star, Justin performs onstage at Acer Arena, Sydney, Australia, April 28, 2011.*

**HE ALSO SPOKE OF A WISH TO "GROW AS AN ARTIST" AND HOPED** his fans would "grow with him." So it was no real surprise when the second episode of *My World* followed so quickly. Featuring fan favorites like "Baby" (with Ludacris), "U Smile" ("that song is amazing!" beamed a proud Justin), and "Eenie Meenie" (with Sean Kingston), it won a GRAMMY Award nomination for Best Pop Vocal Album in 2011. There was also a *My Worlds: Acoustic* release, and, gathering everything together, *My Worlds: The Collection*, which added "Pray" and "Never Say Never" (lending its title to Justin's first movie).

Justin told *Billboard* that the logic behind releasing *My World* in two sections was so that supporters didn't have to wait "over a year and a half" for new tracks. In another interview discussing the more mature and edgy *My World 2.0*, he offered, "I wanted to do something that was a little bit more R&B, and could reach out to everyone. I just wanted to be able to show my vocal abilities." He referred to the first release as his "rookie" album. Reviewers compared the collected set of songs to Michael Jackson, Justin Timberlake, New Edition, and various dance and disco kings.

**ABOVE**
*Ke$ha and Justin onstage at the 52nd GRAMMY Awards, Staples Center, L.A., January 31, 2010.*

**RIGHT**
*Justin and Ludacris perform at the "Saving Ourselves Help for Haiti" Benefit Concert, AmericanAirlines Arena, Miami, February 5, 2010.*

**" I wanted to do something that was a little bit more R&B, and could reach out to everyone. "**
JUSTIN BIEBER

# BIEBER FACTS!

**HIS FAVORITE ALBUMS AS A KID WERE** *THRILLER* **BY MICHAEL JACKSON, AND** *II* **BY BOYZ II MEN.**

Scooter Braun consistently reminded Justin to "get on your Twitter," because "it's how his fans relate to him, and they made him."

Meanwhile the tireless Justin promoted the records extensively on radio and TV, appearing on everything from *Alan Carr: Chatty Man* and *GMTV* in the U.K. to QVC's *Q Sessions*. In the U.S., he guested on *Late Show With David Letterman*, *CBS News* with Katie Couric, and the *2010 Kids' Choice Awards*, as well as big-hitters like *Saturday Night Live* (where he performed a brief comedy skit with *30 Rock* star Tina Fey), the *Today Show*, *American Idol*, and *The Oprah Winfrey Show*. He sang "Bigger" at the MTV Video Music Awards. "I think I'm ready," he muttered enigmatically as the song kicked in. The critic at *Allmusic* applauded his "upbeat, R&B-flavored pop songs" as "light on the ears yet memorable… the unrequited material sounds deeply felt, the ballads have all the necessary us-against-the-world teen-love dramatics." *Entertainment Weekly* cited "real talent" and noticed the "evolution" on the second disc, while *The New York Times* called *My World 2.0* "a seriously good pop record."

*Two superstars together, Beyoncé and Justin share a moment during the 52nd GRAMMY Awards, Staples Center, Los Angeles, January 31, 2010.*

*Sean Kingston and Justin hang out in Miami before the Superbowl kicks off, February 2010.*

**" I want to show that I love to perform. And there are going to be some cool tricks, some electronic things that have never been seen before, for sure. "**

JUSTIN BIEBER

The success of Justin's records just increased fans' desire to see him perform live. And so to their delight, just before *My World 2.0* came out, the *My World* tour—Justin's first—was announced. It ran (in a series of legs, with breaks) from June 2010 right through to October 2011. It began with an extensive North American trek, then crossed Europe, Asia, Australia, and South America. It really was Justin's world. He declared, "I want to show that I love to perform. And there are going to be some cool tricks, some electronic things that haven't been seen before, for sure." He added, "You can expect just to have a great time: it's somewhere that you can just have a blast! It's a place where hopefully you can relate to the songs and stuff. So hopefully you guys will love it!"

Along the way, the tour saw surprise guests joining Justin onstage, from, of course, regular allies Usher and Ludacris to Akon, Shaquille O'Neal, Miley Cyrus, Jaden Smith; Justin's old heroes Craig David and Boyz II Men, and Bow Wow, Soulja Boy, The Wanted, and Chris Brown. And in October 2011, Selena Gomez joined Justin onstage for a duet. Their relationship was to both fascinate Justin's fans and fill many with envy!

**ABOVE**
*Justin makes Jimmy Fallon laugh out loud, April 8, 2010.*

**LEFT**
*Katy Perry and Justin pose for photos at Perez Hilton's "freaky" birthday bash in L.A., March 27, 2010.*

The New York show on August 31, 2010 was filmed for the *Never Say Never* movie, and the October 8, 2011 concert in São Paulo, Brazil, was broadcast on Brazilian television. Not everything went as planned: opening up for his friend Taylor Swift at Wembley Arena, London, he was singing "One Time" when he tripped and broke his foot. Of course he finished his set first—the show must go on—before revealing the extent of his injury. He was in a cast for almost a month. He quipped: "Taylor told me to break a leg last night so I tried. I couldn't break a leg but I broke a foot for you." At least, he added gamely, he would now know what to answer when interviewers asked him for his most embarrassing moment.

Justin was now in a frenzy of demand and was fulfilling a tough schedule of travel and commitments. On the road, he turned up at one Canadian TV station to find a crowd of girls who'd waited five hours just to catch a glimpse of their young idol, singing his songs and chanting his name. And this wasn't

**LEFT**
*Justin belts out his latest hit, "Never Say Never," on the* Today Show, *June 4, 2010.*

**ABOVE**
*JB performing at a sold-out concert at Madison Square Garden, New York, August 31, 2010.*

unusual. Whenever possible, Justin made an effort to find the time to meet and greet his fans and sign autographs and pose for photographs. His team often posted videos of such events on his YouTube channel, and the singer graciously left messages there. In one he said, "Hey guys, it's Justin. I just wanted to add a note thanking you personally for all the support. You are helping a kid from a small town chase a dream, and I am forever grateful. Thanks to you, my family is having a chance at a better life, and I am getting to go and see places I could have never dreamed of."

He added, "This is just the beginning, but I wanted to let you know how thankful I am because without you this would never have happened." Such considerate moments on his Internet presence served to endear Justin to his fans even more. Even some backstage jams while on tour would be filmed and placed online, giving his supporters a look at his working life behind the scenes. On August 4, 2011, he was filmed playing Kanye West's song "Heartless" and Drake's "Successful" on his guitar, and singing them with passion.

He also told *MTV News*, candidly discussing the album, "There's a lot of stuff that's not just about love. There are songs that teens can relate to, as far as parents not being together and divorce and just stuff that happens in everyday life. There are a lot of kids my age and their real life isn't "perfect," everything isn't perfect, so my album kind of portrays that. You just have to make the best of what you have. I'm looking forward to influencing others in a positive way."

RIGHT
*Justin lights up the massive Rio Olympic stadium, October 5, 2011.*

"My message is: you can do anything if you put your mind to it. I grew up below the poverty line; I didn't have as much as other people did." Justin explained that, despite his rigorous schedule, he was still pursuing his education, taking lessons via online classes and with a private tutor. "I want to go to college. I'm good at English, I like to write." When asked where the title *My World* emanated from, Justin replied, "Basically it was the only way I could really describe it! It's so many elements of my world." When an interviewer on Fox's *All Access* show asked him what he really knew about love at his

*Usher and Justin having fun at the American Music Awards, Nokia Theater, L.A., November 21, 2010.*

*" My message is: you can do anything if you put your mind to it. I grew up below the poverty line; I didn't have as much as other people. "*
JUSTIN BIEBER

tender age, Justin answered, "I think it feels good! I mean, I'm not an expert or anything, I'm still learning, I'm still trying to get the process." Lightening up, he laughed, "I'm single and ready to mingle!"

Overall, Justin was adjusting to the heady whirl of fame with impressive balance. "It still feels like a dream. I'm starting to realize this is crazy," he told *Good Morning America*. His mother, on the same show, said, "I feel if there's too much pressure on him, then we scale back and cancel some things, stuff like that. We're just taking it one day at a time." Speaking with CNN, Justin admitted, "It caught me way off guard, it's just been an amazing process. But like I always tell people: what 15-year-old wouldn't want screaming girls waiting for him all the time?" And his advice to those who saw him as a role model? "Just follow your dream. You can do anything you set your mind to. That's basically it!"

**ABOVE**

*Justin and Jack Black get comfy on the U.K.'s The Graham Norton Show, December 7, 2010.*

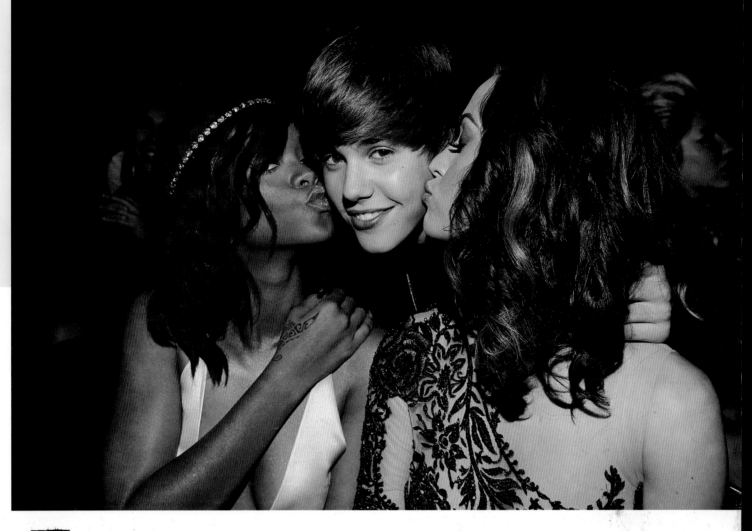

JB's dreams come true as he receives affection from Rihanna and Katy Perry at the MTV Video Music Awards, September 12, 2010.

# BIEBER FACTS!

BELIEBERS—THE BIGGEST FAN BASE IN THE ENTERTAINMENT WORLD—ARE SAID TO MAKE UP A THIRD OF THE EARTH'S POPULATION. ONE BELIEBER PAID $624 FOR A BOTTLE OF WATER THAT JUSTIN HAD TAKEN A SIP FROM.

As the tour stunned and stirred fans around the globe, Justin's dreams were all coming true. "I love being on stage," he said. "I love to see my fans' smiles and hear their screaming because I'm doing something that they want. I really love to perform." How did he see everything progressing? "Five years down the road, I see myself furthering my career—maybe winning a GRAMMY." Well, he came pretty close to that sooner than he expected. Everything was coming up roses for the young man from Stratford, Ontario, who had the world in the palm of his hand. The video for "Baby" had now surpassed Lady Gaga's "Bad Romance" as the most-viewed video on YouTube ever.

He even performed for President Obama and first lady Michelle in Washington, in 2010. The Easter Egg roll is an annual event, held on the lawn of the White House, for children and their parents. Wearing a maroon T-shirt and black jeans, Justin was introduced by Michelle Obama herself, who told the assembled kids, "You can go over to the music stage and have some fun with Justin Bieber. You guys know Justin Bieber?" she joked. "You've heard of him? Well, he's here!" Justin sang "One Time," "U Smile," "Baby," and other songs. He played a drum solo. He surprised the audience with a cover of Run DMC-Aerosmith's "Walk This Way." "What a lovely crowd!" he grinned. "How many of you guys think it's a beautiful day out here? It's a beautiful day!"

Every day was looking pretty good for Justin Bieber now. He took all this in his confident stride. "It was great," he told MTV. "We met [the Obamas], took pictures with them. [The President] was really cool, really nice, and I was just happy to be there."

When *My World 2.0* had raced to number one in the U.S. charts, Justin had tweeted: "Wake up to some incredible news… how do we celebrate? WE DID IT!! I OWE ALL OF U!! THANK U!!"

Beliebers were ecstatic. The *My World* tour gave many of them a chance to see their hero up close and in the flesh and hear him sing the songs they'd swooned to so many times at home. But now they wanted more! Fortunately, Justin was about to offer to take them to the movies, and it wouldn't be long before he'd be touring again, giving them ever-growing reason to believe.

# BIEBER FACTS!

## JUSTIN'S NET WORTH IS ESTIMATED TO BE OVER $130 MILLION.

**RIGHT**
*Justin gets ready for takeoff as he performs during the first night of his U.K. tour at the National Indoor Arena, Birmingham, England, March 4, 2011.*

# NEVER
# SAY
# NEVER

*Never Say Never*, distributed by
Paramount Pictures, was the 3D biopic-
documentary movie that confirmed the
faith of true Beliebers and won Justin a
whole lot of new ones. Described as "the
true story and rare inside look at the rise
of Justin Bieber from street performer in
the small town of Stratford, Ontario to
Internet phenomenon to global superstar,
culminating with a dream sold-out show
at the famed Madison Square Garden."

**RIGHT**
*The Bieber Band backing dancers
get a workout onstage during the
Believe Tour, 2012.*

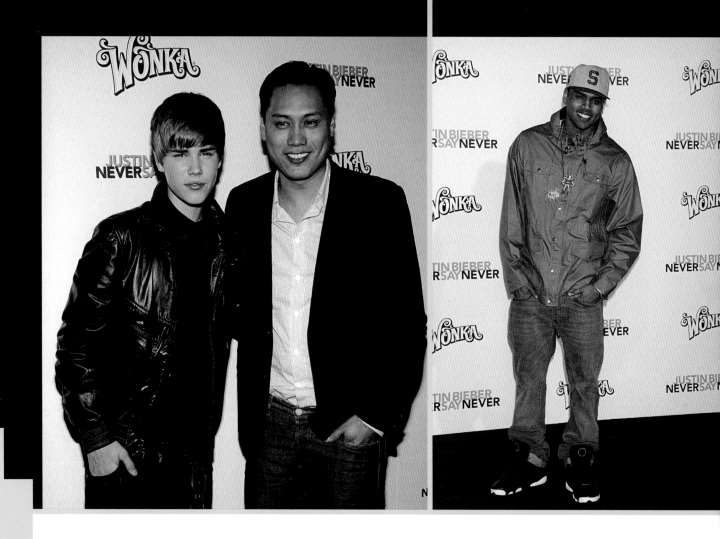

IT WAS DIRECTED BY JON M. CHU—WHO HAS ALSO HELMED JUSTIN'S imminent second movie, *Believe*—and featured Justin, Usher, Scooter Braun, Miley Cyrus, Boyz II Men, and Sean Kingston. Rounding out the amazing cast were Snoop Dogg, Ludacris, Jaden Smith (son of Will and Jada), Mama Jane Smith, Randy Phillips, and Justin's mother Pattie Mallette. There was also archive footage from TV chat shows featuring Justin, guesting with such hosts as Jay Leno, Chelsea Handler, and George Lopez.

Released on February 11, 2011, it boasted the tagline: Find Out What's Possible If You Never Give Up. The movie poster showed Justin standing dressed in black, hands in pockets, in front of a Stratford road sign, declaring his roots.

*Never Say Never* followed the young star in the ten days leading up to his biggest concert up to that point, the New York show of August 31, 2010. (Even in the time since then, he'd gotten bigger and bigger.) The show, where Justin wore his customary tour colors of purple and white, sold out in 20 minutes, and the camera caught footage of thrilled fans at that show and performances from other dates on the *My World* tour. A favorite spot with Beliebers was

**ABOVE LEFT** *Justin and Jon Chu attend the New York movie premiere of Never Say Never, February 2, 2011.*

**ABOVE RIGHT** *Friend Chris Brown is all smiles as he attends the movie premiere of Never Say Never.*

**RIGHT** *JB at a Never Say Never film screening, February 2011.*

**BELOW** *JB on Letterman to promote his film, January 2011.*

" *There's going to be times when people tell you, you can't sell out Madison Square Garden. This is what I tell them: Never say never.* "

JUSTIN BIEBER

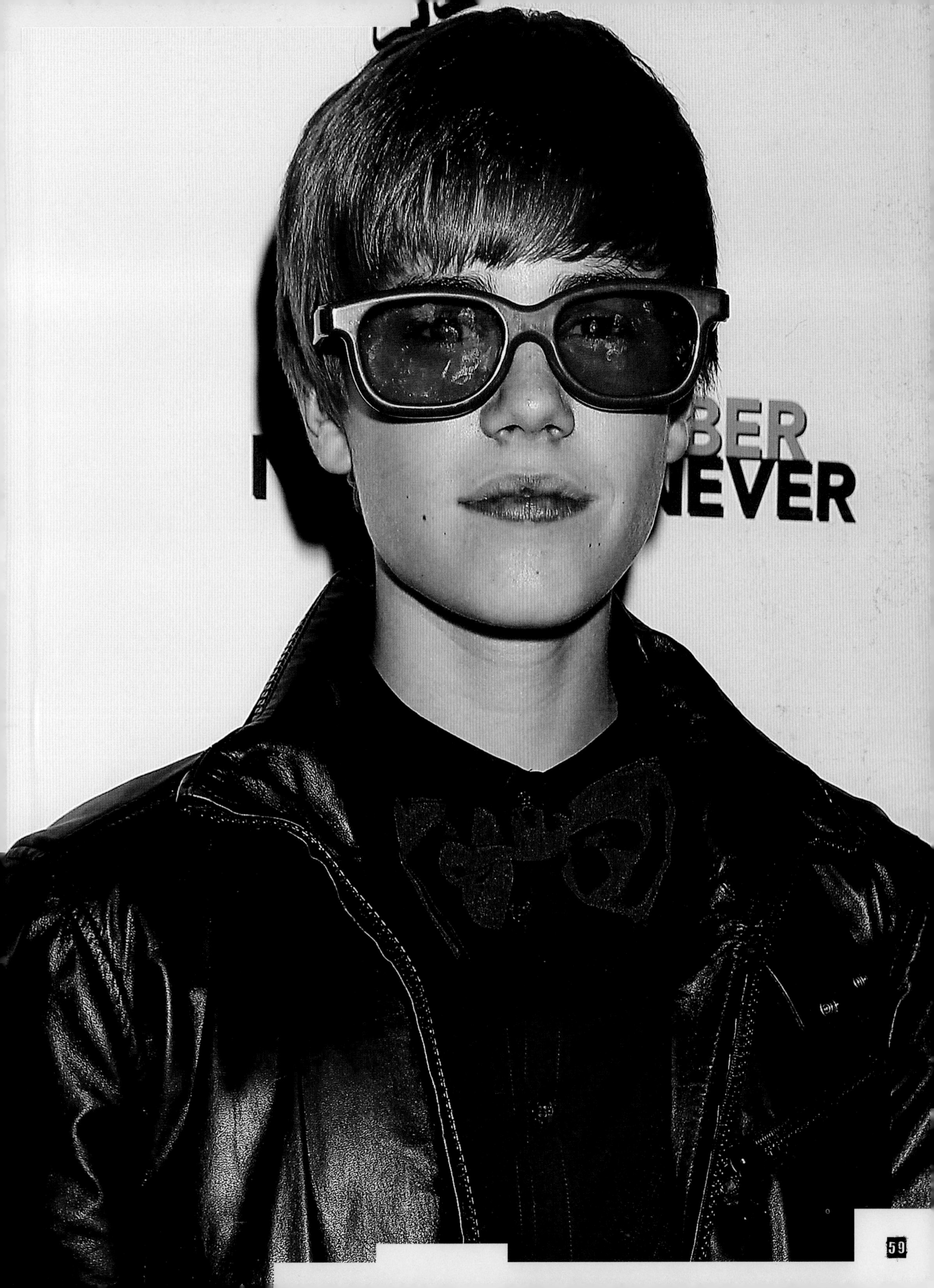
BER
NEVER

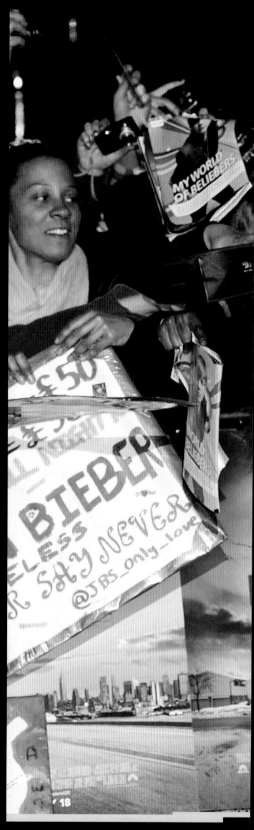

the routine of Justin inviting a girl on stage with him so he could sing "One Less Lonely Girl" to her and gallantly present her with a bouquet of flowers. There were interviews with the people close to Justin, his friends and business associates, though on this occasion no interview with the singer himself. The movie was quite revealing in showing Justin and his team praying together before shows. *MTV News* noted that at the New York show, "Any signs that Bieber had fallen ill only two days before weren't remotely evident. He turned his swag on for the cameras for the upcoming film…"

Another section saw Justin visiting his old hometown of Stratford in Canada, and being reprimanded for not looking after his voice properly while partying with friends. This causes the postponement of a gig in Syracuse and he is required to keep silent, to let his voice heal, for a few days, thankfully recovering in time to play the next show on the tour. There are scenes involving anecdotes about his childhood and his closeness to his mom and to his maternal grandfather, who appears visibly moved when discussing Justin and Pattie's move away from Stratford to Atlanta, Georgia.

The movie's planning and development had fizzed Justin's fans up into a

**LEFT**

*Justin serves snacks to his excited fans ahead of the* Never Say Never *premiere at the O2 Cineworld in London, England, February 16, 2011.*

The U.K. premiere of Never Say Never
in London caused mass Bieber-mania as
hundreds of fans waited many hours to
catch a fleeting glimpse of the star.
February 16, 2011.

state of eager anticipation. The director, who had made the dance-pop-based movie *Step Up 3D*, had announced some of the thinking behind its format, "We had this sort of hyperlink idea through the film, which is what makes it a really interesting movie. It's not like the other concert films where you are onstage and then go backstage… and then onstage and go backstage again." Perhaps Chu's most telling teaser was: "People have a very preconceived notion of Justin Bieber and they can think whatever they want, but we wanted to show honesty—the honest side of Justin."

Justin confirmed the movie's release date on his Twitter account, and that the Madison Square Garden show would be central to it. Chu enthused that he "jumped at the opportunity to tell a story with honesty and heart" and described Justin's tale as a "true underdog story." He added that he'd help tell that tale in a "compelling, genuine way, using all source materials available to convey his path to becoming an icon for this digital age." He also emphasized the fascinating, topical aspects of Justin's rise through YouTube and other digital media, pointing out, "It's a pretty cool story for our time… It's not your typical concert film."

**ABOVE LEFT**
*Rihanna and Justin hang out backstage at the 53rd GRAMMY Awards, L.A., Febuary 13, 2011.*

**ABOVE**
*With Usher at the 53rd GRAMMY Awards, L.A., February 13, 2011.*

**ABOVE RIGHT**
*The name's Bieber, Justin Bieber. JB and CeeLo Green go all glamorous.*

**BELOW RIGHT**
*Rocking the world, one stadium at a time. Justin delights the crowd at the Honda Center, California, October 27, 2010.*

# BIEBER FACTS!

DURING THE SHOOT FOR THE "ONE LESS LONELY GIRL" VIDEO, THE PUPPY RELIEVED ITSELF ON JUSTIN.

That New York show, as witnessed in the movie footage, was very special, with aforementioned luminaries like Miley Cyrus, Justin's friend-mentor Usher, and his boyhood idols Boyz II Men showing up to perform with the new superstar on the block.

Early promotion was unconventional yet effective, with Justin and the director revealing on Twitter that fans could compete to feature in the movie, by sending home movies of themselves singing "That Should Be Me" or a photo or video of their smile. They were given just 24 hours to do so—that didn't stop them from being inundated with entries! In October 2010, Chu set Bieber fans a scavenger hunt puzzle. By solving it, they could find out the movie's title. Ellen DeGeneres and Scooter Braun were among the clue-setters.

While in L.A. signing copies of his memoir *Justin Bieber: First Step 2 Forever: My Story*, Justin spoke about *Never Say Never*. He said one of its motivational aims was to "let people know that there's a lot of people who are discouraging in life, and will tell you, you can't do something, but you just

**" The sky is the limit! "**

JUSTIN BIEBER

got to remember—the sky is the limit! You're able to do whatever you set your mind to as long as you remember to keep God first and stay grounded. I think the movie explains that, and it's really inspiring." His director echoed this with: "Every step, everyone's always said no no no. And he's always said yes yes yes. And that 'never say never' idea is conveyed… to help inspire kids—anyone, kids or adults, really—to follow their dreams."

The trailer, a mix of home and behind-the-scenes clips, emerged on October 26, 2010. *MTV News* praised its "eye-popping visuals" and "sweeping camera moves," declaring it "epic." Justin showed the trailer at his concert in L.A. that night. A subsequent trailer emphasized the 3D effects. These wowed fans when Justin was shown throwing his shirt into the crowd.

*Never Say Never* flew straight to the top of the box office charts, taking 12.4 million dollars on its opening Friday, from 3,105 theaters. By the end of that Bieber-centric weekend, it had grossed 29.5 million dollars. These figures surprised even industry insiders, as it had almost matched the takings of Miley Cyrus' 3D movie of 2008, which had broken records for a music-documentary

**ABOVE LEFT**
*Justin with friends Willow and Jaden Smith, son and daughter of actor Will Smith.*

**LEFT**
*Justin with legendary actor Will Smith.*

**ABOVE**
*Getting all goofy with Russell Brand and Katy Perry at MTV's Video Music Awards in L.A., August 28, 2011.*

# BIEBER FACTS!

## JUSTIN'S OWN PERFUME, NAMED "SOMEBODY," CAME OUT IN JUNE 2011, AND MADE $60 MILLION WITHIN SIX MONTHS.

debut. Justin's movie even out-performed Michael Jackson's *This Is It*, and more than doubled the box office numbers of The Jonas Brothers' 2009 3D movie. It's now become the highest-grossing music concert movie in America for three decades. A limited-release *Director's Fan Cut* came out on February 25, featuring 40 minutes of new footage (while removing 30 minutes of the original edit). The DVD was released in May.

"*Never Say Never* is undeniably entertaining," said critics. They all agreed it would dazzle Justin's fan base, and it certainly did. To their great glee, Justin began hinting at the possibility of a sequel almost immediately. And that dream became reality in January 2013 as the *Believe* movie was announced. The return of Chu as director was a no-brainer. Filming commenced at the concerts at Miami's AmericanAirlines Arena on January 26 and 27. *Believe* was debuted at the Toronto Film Festival in October. Justin used his kidrauhl YouTube channel to preview a teaser trailer, bearing the promise "There's More To This Story." You bet there is!

*" There's more to this story. "*
JUSTIN BIEBER

# UNDER THE MISTLETOE

Santa Claus came to town for Justin's second full studio album, and Beliebers thought all their Christmases had come at once. *Under The Mistletoe* was released by Island Records on November 1, 2011, and raced to number one on the *Billboard* chart. In fact, it was the first Christmas album by a male artist to go straight to number one.

**BELOW**
*Bieber performing in London in November 2011. JB turned on the capital city's Christmas lights during his visit.*

Justin performs onstage at
The X Factor Finale, December
22, 2011, in Hollywood,
California.

Justin gets into the
Christmas spirit on the
Today Show, New York,
November 2011.

Gwyneth Paltrow
presents Justin with the
Golden Deer Award,
and a kiss, at the Bambi
Media Awards ceremony
in Wiesbaden, Germany,
November 2011.

**OVER TWO HUNDRED THOUSAND COPIES WERE SOLD IN THE FIRST** week, and by the end of the year it had already reached almost a million and a quarter sales. This made Justin the first solo artist in the history of pop music to have three number one albums before turning 18.

Justin had broken the news about his new album—a mix of seasonal standards and new Christmas-themed tunes—in late August that year, and soon it emerged that Taylor Swift, Sean Kingston, Usher, Boyz II Men, and producers The Messengers had collaborated. As if that starry list of names wasn't impressive enough, in October, pop superstar Mariah Carey revealed that she and Justin had recorded a duet of her evergreen hit "All I Want For Christmas Is You" for the album. Mariah posted a video online saying, "Justin and I are doing a duet of my song together, which I wrote and produced. I think a lot of you are already very surprised by this—and you're going to be even more surprised when you hear it! The song sounds great. I'm very excited for everybody to hear it this Christmas and to be totally festive with our festive 'collabo.'"

*Justin holds back the emotions at a Christmas show, while on his My World tour, Philips Arena, Atlanta, Georgia, December 23, 2011.*

*Justin performs with Busta Rhymes for the Rockefeller Center Christmas Tree Lighting Special, New York, November 23, 2011.*

# BIEBER FACTS!

JUSTIN'S FAMOUS CHANGE OF HAIRSTYLE IN 2010 WAS DUBBED "THE MOST EXPENSIVE MUSICAL HAIRCUT OF ALL TIME," AS IT MEANT VARIOUS COMMERCIAL PRODUCTS—LIKE JUSTIN DOLLS—HAD TO BE ADJUSTED TO MATCH.

# BIEBER FACTS!

HE GOT HIS FIRST TATTOO IN TORONTO AT 16. HE NOW HAS (AT LEAST) 11, INCLUDING A JAPANESE SYMBOL FOR MUSIC ON HIS RIGHT ARM, A BIRD ON HIS HIP, THE HEBREW WORD FOR JESUS ON HIS RIBCAGE, AND A PICTURE OF JESUS ON HIS RIGHT LEG.

Other festive fillips on the Yuletide special included "Only Thing I Ever Get For Christmas," "The Christmas Song (Chestnuts Roasting On An Open Fire)," "Drummer Boy," "Santa Claus Is Coming To Town," "Home This Christmas," and "Silent Night." "Mr. Bieber hasn't ever sounded this good," claimed *The New York Times*, while the *Guardian* reckoned, "The acoustic 'Silent Night' is most likely to have Beliebers swooning." *Entertainment Weekly* noted some "smooth R&B jangles" and pointed out how unique Justin's raps on "Drummer Boy" were, as he rhymed, "I'm so tight I might go psycho" with "It's Christmastime, so here's a recital…"

Every Bieber fan knew what they were wishing for under the Christmas tree that year…

**ABOVE**
*President Obama takes part in a festive singalong with Justin and Jennifer Hudson at the National Building Museum. Washington, D.C., December 11, 2011.*

**LEFT**
*Performing The Beatles' "Let It Be," Justin sings in the New Year, Times Square, New York, December 31, 2011.*

# BELIEVE

"Justin Bieber is at the top of his vocal game," remarked the *Los Angeles Times* as Justin's third full studio album—*Believe*—was unleashed by Island Records on June 15, 2012. It saw Justin and his team attempting to mature his sound from the "teen-pop" of the two *My World* releases and bring in further elements of contemporary R&B and dance music.

**RIGHT**
*Justin is lowered onto the stage on his famous silver wings, Olympia Hall, Munich, Germany, March 28, 2013.*

**BELOW**
*Performing onstage at the 2013 Billboard Music Awards at the MGM Grand Garden Arena, Las Vegas, May 19, 2013.*

**USHER AND SCOOTER BRAUN AGAIN EXECUTIVE-PRODUCED THE ALBUM** and brought in hit-making collaborators like Max Martin, Hit-Boy, Diplo, and Darkchild. Max Martin was well known for his impressive track record successes with the likes of Britney Spears ("Hit Me Baby One More Time," "Oops… I Did It Again"), Backstreet Boys ("Everybody (Backstreet's Back)"), and Katy Perry ("I Kissed A Girl," "Teenage Dream"). He also co-wrote and produced "We Are Never Ever Getting Back Together" for Justin's friend Taylor Swift.

Hit-Boy had worked with highly credible names like Jay-Z and Kanye West and ASAP Rocky, while Dip-Lo had collaborated with Beyoncé and, of course, Usher. Rodney "Darkchild" Jerkins had enjoyed the honor of working with the late Michael Jackson, as well as Jennifer Lopez, and had won four GRAMMY Awards. The team was strong! Subsequently, *Believe* received plenty of acclaim, with reviewers noting the development and progress within Justin's music. It rocketed straight to number one on the U.S. *Billboard* charts (his fourth), selling 374,000 copies in its first week of release. It soon passed the million mark, going platinum. In Justin's homeland of Canada it went double-platinum, and it made number one in the U.K. (where he was the second youngest male

" *I'm not a fighter by nature, but, if I believe in something, I stand up for it.* "

JUSTIN BIEBER

solo act ever to top the charts). It was also huge in Brazil, Australia, and across Europe. Guest artists included stellar names like Nicki Minaj, Ludacris, Big Sean, and Drake.

Of the five singles from *Believe*, the first was "Boyfriend," co-written by Mike Posner, and it became an American number two and Canadian number one. "As Long As You Love Me" and "Beauty And The Beat" came next, followed by "Right Here" and "All Around The World." In January 2013, the remix album *Believe Acoustic*, featuring three brand new recordings, "Nothing Like Us," "Yellow Raincoat," and "I Would," was released. *Rolling Stone* magazine commented on Justin's "raspy, soulful, vocal tone."

Justin had announced the original album's launch by reappearing on *The Ellen DeGeneres Show* in March 2012. Fans were invited to vote on which of two options for cover art (posted on his website) they preferred. In May he announced the release of a song titled "Turn To You (Mother's Day Dedication)" in honor of Mother's Day, saying that proceeds would go toward

**ABOVE**
*Beliebers get creative and keep the faith with temporary tattoos of their own!*

**LEFT**
*Justin goes all-white during his Believe Tour at Barclays Center, Brooklyn, New York, August 2, 2013.*

**LEFT**
*JB performs at the MGM Grand Garden Arena, Las Vegas, September 30, 2012.*

helping single mothers. Clearly Justin's own upbringing had influenced this generous act.

Reviews of *Believe* praised the stylistic evolution of the more intense beats and the natural strength of Justin's now-deeper vocals. Some noted parallels with Justin Timberlake's career, wherein a teenage boy-band member had metamorphosed into a young adult dance-pop star. *Entertainment Weekly* hailed it as "a reinvention and a reintroduction," observing that the variety of genres made it "the rare album that tries to be everything to everyone and largely succeeds." *The New York Times* credited Justin's instincts and called his voice "limber and wounded" and said he was playing to his strengths. *BBC Music* commended the way Justin understated his confidence and played down his cockiness. Despite this he was never "overshadowed" by his high-quality collaborators. And it suggested great things going forward for the future, as *Billboard* pointed out, hinting "at what Bieber could become someday."

Justin tweeted that he'd been doing a lot of writing, on December 8, 2012. "New stuff—and yeah, the acoustic album, new arrangements—it's

**ABOVE** *Clowning around on* Late Night with Jimmy Fallon, *February 5, 2013.*

**TOP** *JB performs topless in Shanghai, China, October 4, 2013.*

**LEFT** *JB being interviewed on* Late Night with Jimmy Fallon, *February 5, 2013.*

**LEFT**
*Sweet home Canada, Justin brings his show to Fairfax Patriot Center, Vancouver, December 11, 2012.*

**ABOVE**
*Multi-instrumentalist, Justin shows off his drum skills, mid-set on the Believe Tour.*

happening." And so *Believe Acoustic* kept up the momentum. The pared-down versions of the songs, with production trickery removed, revealed "a smoother vocal than most will be familiar with," wrote *Digital Spy*. Bieber fans all have their own favorites, of course: some prefer the dance versions, other the candid acoustic renditions. Most enjoy both, and are happy to hear their hero sing lines in any style!

In February 2013, Justin appeared as both host and musical star guest on legendary TV show *Saturday Night Live*, performing "Nothing Like Us" and "As Long As You Love Me," winning new admirers all the time.

By now, of course, the *Believe Tour*, his second major sojourn, had commenced. It opened in Glendale, Arizona, on September 29, 2012, and Las Vegas the next night. Continuing for over a year, it planned to cover over 150 shows all over the world, crossing continents. Again, Justin chose to announce this news on *The Ellen DeGeneres Show*, proudly stating it would be "the biggest show on Earth." From July, Justin and his crew had begun intense and long rehearsals at the Long Beach Arena in California. He knew he had much to prove and he was determined to offer a truly spectacular concert event each night in every country. Dancers were sought online. Early shows in the U.S. sold out quickly. At Glendale, Justin was understandably sick with nerves but,

like a true trooper, insisted the show must go on. He had to overcome other setbacks and mishaps—at the Tacoma Dome in Washington he tweeted that his laptop and camera were stolen while he was onstage.

After a long American leg through the winter, the tour moved to Europe in February, commencing in Dublin and taking in four controversial nights at London's O2 Arena. As the year went on, Justin played everywhere from Dubai to Johannesburg, Bangkok to Seoul, Buenos Aires to Sydney, still finding time to do another set of American dates. Bieber Fever ran riot! There was quite an array of opening support acts at various venues, too, including Cody Simpson, Carly Rae Jepsen, Mike Posner, The Wanted, Hot Chelle Rae, and Owl City.

Of the opening night in Glendale, despite Justin's anxiety, one reviewer reported that the "show went off without a hitch. Bieber... provided a show that made the cavernous arena seem intimate. Massive amounts of lasers sliced through the 15,000-seat venue, breaking it into several sections." *Variety* magazine said of the Los Angeles show that "his talent is unquestionable... the acoustic tracks allowed for a welcome respite from the sensory overload that characterized the evening. His ambition has never been in question..." Of the same night, the *Hollywood Reporter* opined that "vocally, Bieber shone the most with an acoustic performance of 'Fall,' during which he strummed a guitar while propped up high above the stage," while noting the "high energy, dance

**ABOVE**
*Justin does his favorite Michael Jackson impression live onstage, O2 Arena, London, England, March 4, 2013.*

**RIGHT**
*JB surrounded by adoring fans as he performs at the Barclays Center, New York, August 2, 2013,*

Beliebers in Shanghai, China, get up close and personal with their favorite superstar, October 6, 2013.

"Ladies and Gentleman, this is Captain Bieber speaking. Please fasten your seatbelts!"

moves, pyrotechnics, and audience interaction." Later dates in the tour saw the press mention his "move from pre-teen deity to full-blown cross-generational star." Others just gasped and expressed amazement at what they called the "flash and bang" of the staging and pyrotechnics.

Bieber fans thrilled to hear all their favorite songs. Naturally any setlist is subject to fluctuations, but most nights the evening began in spectacular fashion with "All Around The World." Justin then worked his Beliebers up to fever pitch with the following: "Take You," "Catching Feelings," a medley of "One Time," "Eenie Meenie," and "Somebody To Love," and then "Love Me Like You Do." The show continued with "She Don't Like The Lights," "Beautiful" (sometimes as a duet with Carly Rae Jepsen), "Die In Your Arms," "Out Of Town Girl," "Be Alright," and that acoustic rendition of "Fall." It raced on with "Never Say Never," "Beauty And A Beat," "One Less Lonely Girl," and "As Long As You Love Me," before climaxing—inevitably—with "Believe." For the much-demanded encore, Justin sang the mega-hits "Boyfriend" and "Baby," leaving his fans on a high.

His two nights at Madison Square Garden, New York, at the end of November 2012 particularly impressed both fans and critics. "He still has the charm," declared *The Huffington Post*, "and he put it to good use [at this] sold-out concert." "He showed his vocal strength when singing ballads like 'Catching Feelings,'" offered *The New York Times*, while other write-ups documented him "getting well into his sexy dance moves." A "high-flying performance" of "Be Alright" and the final a cappella note of "As Long As You Love Me" were singled out for praise. The consensus was that Justin was now successfully moving away from his bubble-gum image and keeping audiences engaged as a more mature performer. Fans were, unsurprisingly, "screaming throughout the show!"

BIEBER AIR FLIGHT 777

The U.K. was just as enthusiastic. The Liverpool Echo Arena show of February 25, 2013 garnered a rave review from Jan Tansley, which began, "We already knew he had the face of an angel—now Justin Bieber's got the wings too! And there wasn't one young girl in the Echo Arena last night who didn't think he looked divine. The Canadian superstar descended down onto the stage in the guise of a heavenly creature, and from the moment he landed everyone was floating on Cloud Nine." Justin the "teen giant" had arrived onstage just after 9PM, after a dramatic ten-minute countdown as the girls' screams increased in volume. "Fireworks flared, the music started, and Justin appeared, with his silver wings fashioned out of shining guitars. It was nothing if not spectacular—and just what we have come to expect." Descriptions followed of the hydraulic platform and gadgetry to which Justin attached himself so he could soar above the fans. There were costume changes, from

**ABOVE**

*Do you believe? Justin performs at Barclays Center, Brooklyn, New York, August 2, 2013.*

**CENTER**

*Justin accepts the award for Top Male Artist presented by Miley Cyrus during the 2013 Billboard Music Awards.*

**TOP RIGHT**

*JB reaches out to fans at the HP Pavilion, San Jose, California, June 26, 2013.*

**FAR RIGHT**

*Justin posing with his own Madame Tussauds' wax figure, New York, 2013.*

# BIEBER FACTS!

WAX MODELS OF JUSTIN HAVE BEEN DISPLAYED AT MADAME TUSSAUDS IN LONDON AND NEW YORK.

*Justin makes Whoopi Goldberg very happy during his opening monolgue on Saturday Night Live, New York, February 9, 2013.*

*"I want to tell you I'm so grateful to have each and every one of you in the audience tonight... never in a million years did I think I would have such amazing fans."*

JUSTIN BIEBER

all white to "revealing an increasingly muscular body in black and gold." Justin told his fans, "I want to tell you I'm so grateful to have each and every one of you in the audience tonight... never in a million years did I think I would have such amazing fans. Thank you for supporting me!" As Justin suggested in his chart-topping hit "That Power" with will.i.am: "I can fly, I can fly, I can fly!"

Those who have attended or will attend the *Believe Tour* will never forget it. Christmas was the ideal time of year for Justin's second movie release. The concert-documentary movie *Believe 3D*, the follow-up to *Never Say Never*, hit theater screens on December 25, 2013, a great present for fans. 'Tis the season to be jolly! Justin posted sneak previews and teaser songs (including "Heartbreaker," "Hold Tight," and "All That Matters") online as part of his themed Music Mondays. "I am so excited to be involved in this movie, and so happy to be able to give back to my fans, especially during the holiday season," he has said in a statement. "Jon Chu and my team have done a wonderful job creating a special moment for Beliebers worldwide and I can't wait till Christmas day when the movie will be in theaters everywhere."

Jon Chu, who shot *Never Say Never*, directed again, and Justin co-produced alongside Scooter Braun, Usher, Bill O'Dowd, and Garrett Grant. Scooter and Usher can be seen in the movie, as can Rodney Jerkins, Mike Posner, Ludacris, and others. Scooter, insisting that his company offers global audiences "content that's not only high quality and forward-thinking, but

also authentic," says, "It's no secret that Justin Bieber's name drives a lot of attention. But with *Believe 3D*, we wanted him to tell his own story, truthfully and directly." He vows it will be "better than *Never Say Never*" and has had him "crying and laughing."

*Believe 3D* is a revealing, candid documentary and an explosive record of an enormous—and enormously entertaining—tour, by possibly today's biggest star. There can be no doubt that the movie had many millions of Beliebers crying and laughing along with Justin.

Six years since first being discovered and millions of records sales later, there is just no stopping the multi-talented Justin Bieber. As his amazing story continues, millions of Justin Bieber fans all across the world can't wait to see what he will do next.

**ABOVE**
*Justin shines as he performs to a sold-out show in Brooklyn, New York, August 2, 2013.*

**RIGHT**
*Nicki Minaj and JB perform at the American Music Awards, November 18, 2012.*

# PICTURE CREDITS